CHARLOTTE SONGS

POEMS BY PAUL PINES

MARSH HAWK PRESS | 2015

First Edition 10 9 8 7 6 5 4 3 2 1

Marsh Hawk Press books are published by Poetry Mailing List, Inc.,
a not-for-profit corporation under section 501 (c) 3 United States
Internal Revenue Code.

Cover and interior design by Heather Wood
The text is set in Horley Oldstyle

Publication of this book was supported by a generous grant from the
Community of Literary Magazines and Presses via the New York State
Council on the Arts.

Library of Congress Cataloging-in-Publication Data
Pines, Paul.
[Poems. Selections]
Charlotte songs / by Paul Pines.—First edition.
pages   cm
ISBN 978-0-9906669-7-4 (pbk.).—ISBN 0-9906669-7-2 (pbk.)
I. Title.
PS3566.I522A6 2015   811'.54.—dc23   2015023947

Marsh Hawk Press
P.O. Box 206, East Rockaway, NY 11518-0206
www.marshhawkpress.org

ACKNOWLEDGMENTS

HOTEL MADDEN POEMS: Look Ma, no hands,
Everything my baby; *BREATH*: Stopping at the
bridge, 3 little girls in red, I miss the weeping, Maybe
if we find three wishing stars, *-Daddy, come quickly*,
My daughter, *-Sometimes I call the sky*, GREAT
MAMA SKY, We walk, *"Daddy, I put the sail*, she
wants to know, *Los Pajaros De Jalisco*; *ADRIFT ON
BLINDING LIGHT*: A little girl, A Word About
the Sleep-man, The Man in the Moon, Domes-ticity,
Domestic Navigation; *MARSH HAWK REVIEW*,
The Day Sinatra Died, Recasting Ophelia; *HOME
PLANET NEWS*: Domesticity II, Where The
Yellow Brick Road Ends, The Awkward Years,
Homage To Sextus Empiricus

PAUL BRANTLEY'S "Charlotte Songs" setting
On a green lawn, Maybe if we find
3 wishing stars, She wants to know,
for chorus & piano, premiered by
Young People's Chorus of NYC

To Carol
friend, lover, wife
& mother
of the Poose

CONTENTS

CHARLOTTE
SONGS

PRECOGNITION

Central Park, NYC
June, 1969

A little girl
in a red dress
falls down
in dandelions
laughing at
her own clumsiness

at first
I think her an image
among images then
see she's the whole poem

SNAPSHOTS:
THE FIRST
EIGHT YEARS

1

Look Ma, no hands
I ever imagined

not the ones I thought
would hold me

when my own froze
in a fist or folded

like bad cards
that never pay off

but my daughter's
in the tub

conducting her first
nine months

as if her life were
a symphony

2

– for Charlotte
on her first birthday,
Dec. 28ᵗʰ, 1987

Everything my baby
sees is new

even her daddy
swollen

with the images
and attitudes

of his time
wrapped

in his
love for her

a piñata
she'll open

for the rest
of her life

three little girls in red
on a green lawn
under
a blue sky
hit a rubber ball
with pink paddles
as they argue
over the best way
to do it
and the rules
of the game
and who will get
the ball
when it rolls
into
the bushes

until
they decide
to become
invisible
and
continue
unseen

4

Stopping at the bridge
  over Half-Way Brook

clear water on a sand bed
        such as Hera
        bathes in
        every year
        to renew herself

hers
      the serpent power
      to shed her skin
      become fresh again

and the whole world
  with her...

                  then home
    in time to hear
    my daughter calling
    from the bathroom:

"Daddy, wipe me!"

5

I miss the weeping
   cherry trees
   of Bala Cynwyd

the stream
   by which I raced
   my little girl

while a fist
closed in my chest
as if to say

   "Remember this!"

what is a memory
that anticipates
itself

   a recollection
   that becomes

the ground
on which
the present
plays

   but a breathless

middle aged man
chasing

his four year old
daughter

through
perforations
in the universe

6

"Maybe if we find three wishing stars

we can turn ourselves into

Unicorns

    and fly higher

    than the moon

way beyond

the planet Snoopy

        O Daddy
wouldn't it be fun!

    we could catch comets

    to ride on

because Unicorns are fireproof

and I would have

red patches under

my wings

like a red winged black bird

except I'd be white

and the very last

one alive."

7

-Daddy, come quickly
and bring your knife
death is in the house
I want you to kill him

    -How can I kill death?

-Follow me I'll show you
he's on the second floor
in your study

    -Of course yes I see him
    and is he ugly!

-No you don't
Death is invisible!

    -So show me where he is
    there by the printer?
    Take that...and that!

-Oh Daddy THAT
doesn't hurt him
now he'll kill you

    -No he's perfectly still
    I've done him in

-Be serious Daddy

-I've sliced and diced him
what more can I do?

- You can be harder on him
as hard as you are on me

-Baby I'm not hard on you

- Yes you are but that's okay
you can take your knife
and go back to dinner

-Wait.
I'll give it another try.

-Daddy...really
I know death can't die.

8

My daughter
creeps into bed

between her mother
and myself

shudders
then cries out

at monsters
who surprise her

on the way
to dreamless sleep

I follow her
through gates where

demons wait
all the way down

to that dark embrace
below

thinking
Now I can chart

each step
find my way back

holding on
to her breath

like a
golden thread

9

-*Sometimes I call the sky, GREAT MAMA SKY.*

-And the earth...GREAT DADDY EARTH?

-*No, Daddy. That's MOTHER EARTH.*

-Well, where does Daddy fit in?

-*Maybe, GREAT DADDY SUN?*

-Good. I like that.

-*You know what I call God?*

-What?

-*Sometimes I call God...*
 MR. & MRS. NUSIK.

Sept. 1991

We walk
hand in hand across a lawn
  still green
    to her
    first day of
      Kindergarten
  at Kensington Road School
  this September
    morning

  my heart a leaf
  about to
  fall

    holding on
      until
  she squeezes
    my palm
and says

  "Don't worry, Daddy."

    we
      approach
      our destination
    joined in

what might be
called
    a
    change
    of
    minds

11

"Daddy, I put the sail
　　of the Santa Maria
　　　　on backwards,

　the Nina
　　and the Pinta
　　　are okay but

　the Santa Maria
　　may have to go
　　　to America backwards."

"Do you know what
　　Columbus found when
　　　he arrived?"

"Sure.
　Columbus discovered
　　Glens Falls."

"What else might he
　　have discovered sailing
　　　backwards?"

"That's a hard one, Daddy. Maybe
　that the Indians were
　　already there?"

She wants to know
why I stay up so late

can't make her oatmeal
the way Mommy does

refuse to skip
on our way to school

if reindeer
have soft hooves

is it true Santa
likes my voice so much

we sing Christmas duets
in the living room

and did I really dance
the *cocka-rocha*

with Mariachis
in Guadalajara

and does that explain
why I am the way I am

CHARLOTTE
LA FRANCOPHONE

Paris
June, 30th 1996

She stops half way across

the Pont des Beaux Arts

to say

"Daddy, when I am
a movie star
            I'll have a stretch limo
            you and mommy
            can drive around in it

you'll be all grey
and have a long mustache
going down
with your beard…"

Visiting Fontaine, Normandy

After a breakfast of eggs
in the garden
under a spreading copper
beach
Charlotte looks at what's left
on her plate
          then performs
            a chicken
dance
to expiate her guilt

                    she says
                        for eating
                        my own kind

TRACKING THE MAN
IN THE MOON

A WORD ABOUT THE SLEEP-MAN

I read my daughter stories
the Otoe
told their children
to prepare them for the Sleep Man
explaining how
         coyote became a thief
         little white rabbit got pink eyes
details she will need
to find her way through the landscape
of her life

I'm every father who
tries to explain the seven stars
in the Big Dipper
are also
         seven clans
         (to which she is related)
         seven angels
         seven spirits
         who will advise her in distress
         comfort her in mourning
         join her in celebration

         seven eyes
         that look back in time
         to the place of first things
         where horse and buffalo
         racing to determine who was fastest

left a trail of dust that became
the Milky Way

seven kisses
that wait for her in heaven
where all events are marked
before they are recorded

"Yah-wah shee-geh!"

THE MAN IN THE MOON

The story goes that Running Antelope
became the Man in the Moon
trying to rescue his wife Little Hill
abducted by a wicked Chief
whose power proved so great
that the Water Spirit
had to help the brave escape
into the night sky

I ask myself
if Running Antelope
still searches for his wife
wonders if she misses him
does she recognize his face
gazing down
and take comfort

looking at my daughter
and my wife asleep
I know the answer
recognize my own face
as the one
reflected
in water

DOMESTICITY

Zorro by the door chews his bone
Ben Webster on NPR
plays *Making Whoopee*
my wife in the bedroom talks
on the phone

I recall other lives
on the lower East Side
in Cholon
nights in smoky clubs
listening to Eddie Jefferson
wandering Belizean bush
over empires buried
under half an inch
of earth...

    until my daughter
    wonders what I'm doing
    alone in the dark
    asks, *Daddy, are you all right?*

   Sure, I say

     knowing she's afraid
     I've gone too far away
     and might never
     come back

DOMESTIC NAVIGATION

1)

- When you were away
I realized to what degree
I depend on you and Charlotte
to navigate
       like stars
in my heaven I need you
to triangulate
        my position

Carol touches my hand
        not that I didn't enjoy
        the trip alone to Stowe
        and the concert
        but I felt so adrift
        in the motel room looking
        for you and...

Charlotte later asks me
to help her paste glow-in-the-dark stars
on her bedroom ceiling
standing on a chair
I arrange The Little Dipper
at her direction spacing
handle and bowl
just so

days go by
then one morning
she invites me to witness
the glory of her heaven
having added several
constellations
of her own

     a heart
     her initials
     a smiley face

and an incomplete
Orion
     with a space
     in his skirt
     - Where he pooted

2)

Eric arrives from NYC
beat by the car trip
                and a bad meal in Malta
collapses on the couch half asleep
but wakes long enough
to inform us of discoveries concerning the great pyramid
and its astronomical alignments
                        how the three stars in Orion's belt
                        line up with a tunnel leading to
                        a secret chamber to produce
                        a moment of singular energy
                        that will make anyone in it
                        immortal
                unlike
Charlotte's universe
carefully configured on her bedroom ceiling
where the very same stars
essential to such important work
are blown away
every time the Hunter
passes gas

THE DAY SINATRA DIED

In the shower I wash my thinning hair
threads that connect me
  to the invisible
guide me through the daily labyrinth
of a beastly
world

>   wonder that so much of it
>   has come off in my brush

>   and how I will navigate
>   my daughter's future
>   when it's gone

>   (poor Ariadne
>   deserted by her hero)

she calls
through the door
"Daddy, Zorro has snot on his paw
but I've wiped it off..."

>   "On what?"
>   I ask

gathering my clothes
suddenly worried about her next year
at Middle School

>   and how to handle
>   a dog with
>   a nose
>   cold

SECRET AGENTS

Five days from elementary school graduation
Charlotte wants to eat breakfast at McDonalds

as we did when she was a child who asked me
to cut her sausage in "little bird pieces"

so she could nibble them between bites
of her biscuit

                as she does so again I am struck
                by how beautiful she's become
                her long ballerina neck
                hair pulled back
                in a bun

                how womanly she seems
                brushing crumbs
                from her cheek before
                pointing at a man
                with a ginger mustache
                who leaves two brief cases
                by the Men's Room door
                then disappears
                inside

"He's a rebel. He doesn't floss."

she continues to chew
and sip OJ as the first man is followed by a second

in a blue suit.

"He's a rebel too. Doesn't brush."

The first man comes out
grabs a brief case, goes back in.

Five minutes later the blue suit exits
followed by the sound
of the air dryer.

"Repairmen," I say.

"Secret Agents," she whispers.

"You think?"

"No, Daddy. It's a game we play
at school...except Sara and Tara
refuse to die. I shoot them
but they won't fall down."

We trash the plastic. On the way out she wants to know
if I remember who sang
I See A Pale Moon Rising.
I don't but hum it
until we pull up in front of a red brick
building surrounded by a deep green lawn

of the wettest June on record
where she gets out
and I watch her back pack bounce
then disappear through
glass doors

THE DUALIST

When my daughter
graduated from
elementary
school

as I watched
my tomatoes redden
after a month
of rain

and again
last night when my wife
reached across the pillow to
hug me then whispered
  It's hard to believe
  we're over fifty
  isn't it?

          I said
          No
          but thought
          It is always so

when my daughter
returned with her hair
in corn rows

as I watched

my tomatoes ripen
after another
heavy rain

and again
last night
when my wife reached across
our pillow

    I said
    at birth we leave
    our essence
    in another sphere
    a pure idea
    which comes to meet us
    after death

        one
        we always knew
        approaches

        one
        we recognize
        right away
        in a body of
        light

    the same

one

    we felt present
    in the shadow
    of events

as radiant

sorrow

FAMILY ROAD TRIP

Approaching Montreal
we see the dome of St. Joseph's Oratory
golden in the setting sun

> eleven year old Charlotte
> between bucket seats
> holding the surprise
> in her Happy Meal
> says,
> > *-This is Mr. Flotation Device*

a plastic donut
with inflated arms, legs, and turtle head
around a flat center useful
as a floating ashtray

> *-Why does he have three eyes?*
> asks my wife

> *-Because HE's enlightened*
> Charlotte elevates him
> like the Host

then places him on my head
like a hat

> *-Get that thing off me!* I tell her

-Apologize to Mr. Flotation Device, she insists.
Tell him you love him, and are sorry.

> *-Sorry,* I say, to keep the peace.

Mr. Flotation Device responds with an inflatable raspberry
-*You're not sincere*
she accuses in a faux French accent.

Approaching the Champlain Bridge
he's back on my head.

-*Mr. Flotation Device can also suck the enlightenment*
out of you.

I hear a sound that approximates a slurpy
sucked through a straw.

-*And now the same for Mommy, unless you say*
I love you and I'm sorry.
And be sincere!
Good Mommy. Mr. Flotation Device
can also put enlightenment back
into your head,

which entails noises associated with sustained
electrical vibration.
-*Your enlightenment is back.*
And here is some of Daddy's. He doesn't need it
anymore!

As we turn off to Iles de Soeurs
I hear myself call out,

-I'm sorry Mr. Floatation Device
this time I really mean it. Will I ever be
the same again?

-Don't worry, replies The Translucent One
hovering between our seats. *I've been there*
in negative numbers myself

                                    -What happened?
-I had to sit in a bowl of rice
for two years.
                        -That must have been difficult.

-More than that...I ate the rice and became enlightened,
only to wind up in a Happy Meal!

ILES DE SOEURS

From Ruth's 11th floor balcony
overlooking the St. Lawrence
the lights of Montreal
at night float on
the river

          the interior is white
          carpets
          and mirrors
          porcelain in glass cabinets
          pictures of weddings
          her two husbands
          children
          and grand children
          pink carnations
          in boxes
          a glass table
          surrounded by white chairs
          LOVERS IN ART
          on the coffee table...

she welcomes us
as house guests
my eleven year old daughter
looks around
and asks

       -If you had a choice
       which would you choose,
       to be locked in or out of here?

IN CONFINIO MORTIS

In Quebec City
high above the St. Lawrence
we walk the Plains of Abraham
discover the Joan of Arc Memorial Garden
a few feet from the Place de Montcalm
My wife samples lemon thyme
that grows along the path
crushing purple buds
in her palm
        which Charlotte sniffs
        then opens wide
        her eleven years old eyes
        and exclaims
        in a semi southern
        drawl:

                -Oh my little Joany
                would have loved this!

DOMESTICITY II

Hard getting out of bed this morning
the day's obligations loom

call

the plumber
doctor

remember

Charlotte's Youth Theater performance
at the mall

I walk out of the bedroom on sore feet
pass my wife at the computer playing solitaire

in the bathroom I'm suddenly alone
with all the essays and poems
I'll never write

turn on the tap
and remember
last night's dream
about

Chinese girls
kneeling by a stream
along the Silk Route
sipping water from
hands like
tea cups

WHERE THE YELLOW BRICKS END

1)

The Lake George Youth Theater
mounts a production of The Wizard of Oz
in the high school auditorium
without air conditioning
in spite of which I'm reminded

> Frank L. Baum
> penned what might be
> the quintessential
> American myth
> in the 20's

and here at the century's end
these kids are playing it
back again

> a drama in which the childlike soul of Democracy
> from the heartland meets
> the undeveloped aspects
> of a populous

> > in search of a heart
> > head
> > and the courage
> > of their convictions

over a hundred of us
melting in our seats watch Democracy
set off again on a road paved with gold

fleeing a tyrannical witch through the haunted wood
to find an Emerald Kingdom dominated by
a bogus Wizard which she unmasks
to the joy of everyone

                    as if to revise Locke's
                    view of man in his natural state
                    homo homini munchkin

2)

my *munchkin* daughter
for whose sake I brave the airless room
welcomes Democracy

                    a kid in ruby slippers
                    who will later struggle to remember
                    why the companions in her dream
                    seem familiar
before collapsing in a poppy field
to sink even deeper

                    into a dream within
                    a dream
until the good witch intervenes
with a sobering snow fall
and the bad witch
laments

-There's nothing so depressing
as boundless optimism.

as she melts into the floor boards
this woman who devours
dogs and children
on the threshold
of extinction
exclaims

> *-Who would have thought a little girl*
> *could destroy my beautiful wickedness!*

Even so we know it is not over
that Dorothy Democracy must find her way home
to a nation which must
learn to veer away from obesity
honor poets
eliminate ghettos
respect the mentally ill
and disabled

3)

all through the curtain calls
and standing ovation
I repeat,

> *-No! It's not over!*

This is no time for curtain calls!
We are still afflicted
by the generational transmission of abuse
the implications of the death penalty
wounded vets trailing PTSD like red paint
on our Yellow Bricks...

Outside in the street kids in grease paint
hug their parents

        cars honk
        all of us breathless
        at the dawn of a new century

until an invisible gate keeper
standing at the bars
of an invisible gate whispers
in my ear:

        If there were no wizard
        why would you
        be here?

A RIVER
THAT FLOWS
BOTH WAYS

THE AWKWARD YEARS

Sixteen-year-old Charlotte
in back of the van closes her math book
then comments that her friend Caitlin
shares her dark humor.

"She's the only one who laughs
at my dead baby jokes."

My wife in the passenger seat
presses an invisible brake
while I make no attempt to fill
the silence.

       "What's funnier
than a dead baby?" Charlotte asks,
then answers:
       "A dead baby
       in a clown suit."

Our daughter's laughter shatters
like a dropped wine glass.
Her mother leans forward
to pick up the pieces

I watch our baby
in the rear view mirror
presiding at her own
wake.

GRAND DESIGN

Charlotte isn't sure
she wants to be an actress anymore

there are too many talented people
waiting tables

instead she'll open a restaurant
of her own

The Wiggle Room

where patrons will breakfast
on waffles in pumpkin butter

served by four waiters dressed
as dancing omelets

belting out a du wop version of
"Oh What A Feeling"

EMAIL FROM THE GRAMMAR MONSTER

hello, daddy!! how are you?
i am well, thank you.
i won't beat around the bush.
i have a very serious question for you...
really more like a request.
you know my friend dominique?
well, if you don't, you should.
I have told you about her.
anyway, she has gotten herself
into a sort of predicament.
she asked me if i knew any psychics
and i thought of lisa.
dominique goes down to the city
regularly and was wondering if
i could refer her to lisa.
if you could ask lisa or give me
her number to give to dominique,
that would be uber-cool.
love, your daughter
whom you love so much

MEET MY DAUGHTER DIMITRI,
THE EVIL COMMUNIST DICTATOR

My 16 year old daughter Charlotte
insists that from now on she

will answer only to the name of Dimitri
in her own brand of *Sovietski*

which features such words as da,
nyet and *spacebo*. At her request

we drive to the Price Chopper
for low carb candy bars (*very good for*

losing weightski) because Dimitri
has decided to go on the Atkins *dietski*

which for her means chicken fingers
and turkey burgers since she is

otherwise a *wegetarian* who can't
stand mushrooms, peppers, onions

and all the traitorous *legumskis.*
Oh shitski, she cries in front of

the store. *Not socks with shorts!*
Dadski what could you be thinking.

Holy Pirogi, worse still, with sandals!
Have you no shameski? Please,

I protest. This is perfectly acceptable
in most circles. *Nyet! Nyet! Nyet!*

Evil communist dictator daughter
knows. They will not even let you

into the Gulag wearing socks
with sandals. Shapeupski.

But Lenin, I insist, always wore socks
and sandals. So did Trotsky, which is

why Frida Kahlo fell in love with him.
She said, *Oh Leon, my Lion, I simply*

can't get enough of those holy argyles
sticking out of your huaraches!

This stops her, but only for a moment.
Dadski, you lie! For punishment

you must memorize all of Pushkin
while listening to Russian hip-hopski.

In the organic food aisle, Dimitri
conducts a survey of shoppers

who agree that socks with sandals
is probably a reactionary hold over

from *days of the Czar* , points me out
to the cashier as an inbred Romanoff

with hemophilia *and* bad taste
The cashier smiles, *Credit or Debit?*

To which Dimitri replies, *You will*
spend July reading Dr. Zhivago.

Evil communist dictator follows me
to the van frowning at my feet.

I am relieved when later that night
after instant messaging her cohort

Vladimir in Palo Alto she offers
to sing me Soviet Lullabies they have

composed to the tunes of *Oh Canada*
and *Somewhere over the Rainbow.*

MATCHSTICK MAN

On our way to college at New Paltz
Charlotte points to a house

with a sagging porch and sighs,
"Daddy, you once said

the Seven Dwarfs were buried
under those lawn ornaments.

For years I really believed
the Seven Dwarfs were dead

and buried in West Glens Falls!
What other lies have you told me?"

ON THE WING
WITH MOTHRA

HOMAGE TO SEXTUS EMPIRICUS

1

Philosophy
brings her so much
pleasure
Charlotte has considered
Switching her major
From musical theater
To an equally insupportable one
and sends me
a text message signed
Sextus Empiricus

> *in our*
> *individual*
> *peculiarities*
> *we differ in*
> *such a way*
> *that some*
> *people digest*
> *beef more*
> *easily than*
> *rock-fish, and*
> *get diarrhea*
> *from weak*
> *Lesbian wine*

To which I respond

that while she might
go to sleep with the Stoics
she will probably
wake up
with Skeptics

2

Charlotte calls me
to explain
her latest message from Sextus
points to differences
between people and behaviors
that make it
difficult to draw hard
or fast
conclusions:

> "He (Sextus)
> Goes on to talk about
> Tibido the Roman
> a soldier who
> eats human brains
> We don't know much more
> about him (Tibido) who
> like so many others
> remains lost

in the mists
of history."

today I find another text
in which she
again cites (Sextus)
the authority
on keeping
an open
mind

        "Some people
        say they would
        rather eat
        their father's head
        than beans."

RECASTING OPHELIA

I'd say that time
and space conspire

to create impediments
but that sounds

too much like
Polonius

whose speeches
last summer

were cold comfort
watching Charlotte

go mad as Ophelia
end every evening

on stage at Saratoga
Shakespeare

in a coffin too hard
watching her die

the summer before
in *Les Mis* my baby

Eponine a mortally
wounded robin

on the barricade
singing her rain-song

and now off stage
haunted by fears

she is trapped
in the water soaked

weight of Ophelia's
robes eyes staring

out her window
at a willow wilting

in the winter light
makes me cry

I worry about her
living so far away

in Brooklyn
blocks from where I

grew up my Eponine
passing guys

on stoops who whistle
and call out:

How's it goin'
Snow Flake?

Dear Charlotte,

There is no getting around it this year, the wassail was
an issue. Your dad insisted we review carols that Vlad
the Impaler might've sung to his serfs, soldiers, as well
as enemies at the siege wall. I'm no prude but I draw the
line at *Whose nuts are roasting on an open fire?* and *I'll be
bone for Christmas*. It's not that I'm particularly politi-
cally correct, but I'm really uncomfortable with *Rudolph
the headless reindeer*, or *Cartilage in a pear tree*. He looked
hurt when I questioned his message. In addition to which
he was reluctant to sing full voice through his bronchitis.

"Not much support from the puffer," he said.

I told him to stop being self-indulgent.

He threatened to spike my egg nog with Prednisone.

I tried to be gentle with him. Obviously, he was off
his game, even something of a sourpuss. But he served
the wonderful cider you made and that cheered us both
up. Then he told me about your triumphant senior year
at New Paltz, singing the lead in *Urinetown* and *Pirates*.
It brought a light to his eyes. He was especially excited
by your Marta, in Sondheim's *Company*. He says you had
to dig deep to make her live—*no shtick*, is how he put it.
Then, your essay in response to Prof. Appleboom?
A good name for a philosopher—brings to mind the tree
in the garden. Knowledge means more mess, but more
awareness too and that's a good trade. It's called "growing
up." He is so proud of the way you are doing this.

I agree, and add my pride which spans poles and goes up and down chimneys. I remain, as always, your biggest fan.

Love,
Santa

EPIPHANY

1

Charlotte dreams we meet in a Synagogue
she's already there when I come in
when asked if she is Jewish
she gestures half and half then
points at me and says,
"But He Is"

> At a window
> she sees two young men
> splashing in a fountain
> mountains distant
> sunshine in the water
>
> they yell,
>   "So it won't be,"
> at a girl in the window
> who (she) corrects
> their grammar to mean
> the opposite
>
> as if uttered at the end
> of a Wicca ceremony
>
> *So it mote be!*

2

A parade of giraffes
pink ones on roller skates
pass for review
her attention is riveted
By a jewel encrusted one
In an Elizabethan collar
standing on
two feet

       against a jewel encrusted
       wall she can't
       get over

           how poised
           he is

VOICE LESSON

We congratulate Charlotte on her first
theatrical review in the *N.Y. Times*

responding to her performance as
a Magical Being sent from Olympus

to celebrate the first sexual encounter
of a middle aged Chinese American

comedian who suffers from Asperger's
and OCD she is called "delightful"

and "enchanting" a perfect foil for a
petulant neurotic male she recites it

on the way to her Crown Heights
apartment then breaks into song

"…crying cockles and muscles
alive, a-live O," to which her mother

points out that in the second verse
Sweet Molly Malone dies of a fever

from which "no one could save her"
probably a suspicious "cockle or muscle"

while her ghost continues to push
a wheel barrow through narrow streets

which is sad and not at all Charlotte's
fate. "Poor thing," says our girl. "No

doubt she was in the wrong line of work
for one severely allergic to shell fish."

AMOR & PSYCHE

My daughter who has carried
her parent's unfulfilled fantasies

since she was a child (she is
so beautiful how could it be

otherwise) her dark eyes
voiced to silence all others

the quality of her attention
that of a robin on a wire

listening for worms
retreats into a crystal castle

served by invisibles
who whisper kind words

where she waits for the lover
whose face she can't see

a wintergreen breath
that comes at night or by

day an odor on the wind
until she grows bored

with too much safety
impatient to see love's shape

allows her secret place
to dissolve into a resonance

which will return to her
now and then for the rest

of her life as birdsong
or wintergreen on the wind...

ADIOS

LOS PAJAROS DE JALISCO

The birds of Guadalajara
pajaros in the Plaza
de los Mariachis

corvo ^
   tordo ^
      ^   *golandrina*
            ^

are the same birds
   I heard in Menemsha
      and Glens Falls

            in Bala Cynwyd
               and outside our bedroom
                  on the Rue Bievre

      the very birds
      that sang to Plato
   and Aristophanes

   the Venerable Bede
      Torquemada
         my father in Galicia

crow ^
   thrush ^
      ^   *swallow*
            ^

will sing
our daughter awake
after I am gone

∧

listen for me
Charlotte
in their song

Dear Charlotte—I have a chance to publish this book
and think it a good time to do so, but won't without your
green light. With that in mind, I've listed options which
cover possible responses that will eliminate any awkward
apologies or explanations. Simply pick a number and that
will be the answer.

POSSIBLE RESPONSES TO PUBLISHING
CHARLOTTE SONGS:

1) Go For It Daddy!
2) I need to think about it
3) No!
4) I don't want to deal with this now (or ever).

PAUL PINES grew up in Brooklyn around the corner from Ebbet's Field and passed the early 60s on the Lower East Side of New York. He shipped out as a Merchant Seaman, spending part of 65/66 in Vietnam, after which he drove a cab until opening his Bowery jazz club The Tin Palace, the setting for his novel, *The Tin Angel* (Morrow, 1983). *Redemption* (Editions du Rocher, 1997), a second novel, is set against the genocide of Guatemalan Mayans. *My Brother's Madness* (Curbstone Press, 2007), a memoir, explores the unfolding of intertwined lives.

He has published twelve books of poetry: *Onion, Hotel Madden Poems, Pines Songs, Breath, Adrift on Blinding Light, Taxidancing, Last Call at the Tin Palace, Reflections in a Smoking Mirror, Divine Madness, New Orleans Variations & Paris Ouroboros, Fishing On The Pole Star* and *Message From The Memoirist.* Poems set by composer Daniel Asia appear on the Summit label, and opposite Israeli poet Yehuda Amichai, in his 5th Symphony recorded by the Pilsen Symphony. Pines is the editor of the Juan Gelman's selected poems translated by Hardie St. Martin, *Dark Times/ Filled with Light* (Open Letters Press, 2012). He lives with his wife, Carol, in Glens Falls, NY, where he practices as a psychotherapist and hosts the Lake George Jazz Weekend.

paulpines.squarespace.com
www.paulpines.com
www.tinangelopera.com
www.versedaily.org/2013/aboutpaulpines.shtml

COMMENTS ON OTHER BOOKS BY PAUL PINES

MY BROTHER'S MADNESS

My Brother's Madness is part thriller, part an exploration that not only describes the causes, character, and journey of mental illness, but also makes sense of it. It is ultimately a story of our own humanity.
                                                    —*KIRKUS REVIEW*

Take what pain, hope, sorrow, and madness there is in this world, pass it through the alembic of an educated sensibility and a deep, informed compassion, and you might be lucky enough to reach *My Brother's Madness*.
                —JAMES HOLLIS, JUNGIAN ANALYST, & AUTHOR OF
                        WHY GOOD PEOPLE DO BAD THINGS

THE TIN ANGEL

This swift tale of murder and revenge rattled along stylishly and fulfills all our expectations for high-grade suspense.
                                    —*THE NEW YORK TIMES BOOK REVIEW.*

Superb...enough terror, suspense, and low-life atmosphere to keep the most jaded hard-boiled enthusiast happy.
                                        —*THE WASHINGTON POST*

I haven't read a grittier mystery in years, or—I suspect—a
truer one. —NY DAILY NEWS

THE HOTEL MADDEN POEMS

Hotel Madden is a fine and powerful book. —WILLIAM BRONK

Paul Pines' dedication to *Hotel Madden Poems* describes
the book as a "fugue." That's exactly what this brilliant and
compelling work is...

        —LAWRENCE JOSEPH, *AMERICAN BOOK REVIEW*

BREATH

...the Poems in Breath constitute a heartfelt, extended medita-
tion on the transporting effects of everyday phenomena, how
the psychic wormholes that allow and instantaneous travel
along our internal galaxies hide just underneath the next
memory, the next sentence, and behind the all, the ALL
itself—unknowable, perhaps, but in Pines' poetry nearly
imaginable.

        —FRED MURATORI, *THE AMERICAN BOOK REVIEW*

ADRIFT ON BLINDING LIGHT

Pines take the reader on a mysterious complicated journey.
Dreams, archetypes, icons, friends and confessions swirl
through the poems in beautiful and complex images...This
wonderfully unpredictable, intuitive book navigates the
conscious and subconscious worlds with fluid, imaginative, and
fascinating energy--as poets should do.

        —WILLIAM KELLY, *MULTICULTURAL REVIEW*

Adrift on Blinding Light is full of exquisite moments; of words and phrases that have been mined by the author like gems and presented to us with the sense of wonder they engender and deserve. —LEE BELLAVANCE, *THE CAFÉ REVIEW*

Paul Pines' latest book, *Adrift on Blinding Light*, offers a dazzling tour through a poet's selfconstruction…although these images may not raise us up in the emotional sense, they always seem to arrive as a startling surprise, perfectly timed to shake us out of the ordinary. —NEIL KOZOLOWICZ, *RAIN TAXI*

Paul Pines is a latter-day pioneer of feeling, in one verse aiming to write a poem of last words; in another finding and using the single word reverberating "through which/ to approach/ what remains unexplored." *Adrift on Blinding Light* is a book of brilliant insights and lyrical sadness, and of a mod est hard-headedness that will stay in the mind.
—CORINNE ROBINS, *THE AMERICAN BOOK REVIEW*

TAXIDANCING

Reading Pines is not unlike listening to good jazz. The poems are strangely emblematic allowing us to progressively come into their world, becoming, as we go, increasingly hip and eager to hear their urgencies. —JULIA CONNER, *FIRST INTENSITY*

What a background for a poet. Paul Pines grew up in Brooklyn, and spent time in the Lower East Side of NYC. He tended bar, drove a cab, shipped out as a merchant seaman, and opened his own jazz club in the Bowery:"The Tin Palace" in 1970. He is now a practicing psychotherapist in upstate New York. So this ain't your usual MFA-trained bard, but certainly one who has been well-schooled. Hugely Recommended.

—DOUG HOLDER, BOSTON AREA SMALL PRESS AND SCENE

LAST CALL AT THE TIN PALACE

Thank you, Paul Pines, for a sublime ride! —DAVID MELTZER

...the poems are magical, revealing, yet personal, and all the time—engaging. *Last Last Call at the Tin Palace* delivers.
—BRIAN GILMORE, *JAZZ TIMES*

Yet for all the ecstasy there is also elegy and the recorder of past lives must blaze a trail of tears as well as paths of illumination.
—JON CURLY, *RAINTAXI*

Last Call at the Tin Palace, by Paul Pines...poems that are stories that are jazz that are memories that are everlasting imprints of music on retinas...
—BOB HOLMAN, POETRY PICKS, THE BEST BOOKS OF 2009

REFLECTIONS IN A SMOKING MIRROR

What ties these poems together is Pines' distinctive voice and the omnipresent guide of his demanding and imposing perspective. Pines makes the past his own and with each subsequent line owns whatever time is spent savoring his poems.
—ERIC HOFFMAN, *BIG BRIDGE #16*

The only other person I can compare this to is Goethe...
Powerful stuff! —PAUL ELISHA, *NPR-WAMC*

These poems are similar to a Keith Jarret Concert. They can rip your heart out and leave the reader defenseless.
—DOUG HOLDER, *BOSTON AREA SMALL PRESS AND SCENE.*

Merely stating that the book proved "insightful" doesn't do justice to the unexpected expansion of consciousness.

—*Jottings of an AmeriQuebeckian*

I keep finding new layers of meaning couched between lines... poems like "Restaurant Villa Hermosa," "Vectors," "Reflections in a Smoking Mirror," and "Birds of Belize II" grab hold of me and don't let me go.

—Cameron Scott, *Sugar Mule #36*

DIVINE MADNESS

Now, in 2012, Pines suggests that, like The Serpent in the Bird, there are "gods" inside the minds of men. How creative and brilliant, yet how disconcerting at the same time.

—Pam Rosenblatt,
Boston Area Small Press and Scene

Paul Pines's *Divine Madness*, an empathic scatting to the music of the spheres that seems to sound simultaneously from both the deepest interior of human consciousness and the farthest reach of the celestial dome.

—Fred Muratori, *The Notre Dame Review*

In modes as diverse as the crime novel (The Tin Angel), the memoir (My Brother's Madness), opera, and eight volumes of poetry, Pines pursues-with keen and nuanced observation-the psyche's flights, fissures, mania, and brilliance.

—Naftali Rottenstreich, *Big Bridge #17*

Pines has distilled a lifetime of reading, thinking, caring, and writing into *Divine Madness*. It is indeed divinest sense.

—Norman Finkelstein, *JACKET 2*

NEW ORLEANS VARIATIONS
& PARIS OUROBOROS

...some of the most memorable and finely wrought poems of anybody on the scene today...

—Louis Proyect, *The Unrepentent Marxist*

His [Pines'] chiseled reveries are insightful yet affecting in their sheer presence...

—Burt Kimmelman, *Golden Handcuffs Review*

With his latest Paul Pines reveals himself to be at the peak of his poetic powers...the movements across and between a multiplicity of reference is just fabulous...the collection is a wonderful manifestation of something he quotes from Homer: "We leave home to find ourselves."

—Eileen Tabios, *Galatea Resurrects #21*

FISHING ON THE POLE STAR

Have writer's block or artistic ennui? Find yourself bereft of inspiration and adrift in life's doldrums? My advice: go fishing! Even better, get Paul Pines' new book of poems, Fishing on the Pole Star...Pines turns this wonderfully chronicled fishing voyage with a family of friends through the Bahamian isles inward, across lines of deeper self-knowledge and surprising allegory. Dream-like collages and a contrast of gorgeous maps, both antique and modern, add a soulful surrealism that seems magically appropriate. —Dennis Daly,

Wilderness House Literary Review 9/3

Fishing on the Pole Star is full of wonder, for Pines knows that fishing correlates with the Arthurian Graal-search, the poet's hunt for the poem, the deep sea-voyage to heal the wounded soul. This collection places him in the tradition of Hektorovi, Walton, Melville, Hemingway, and Hughes.

—RICHARD BERNGARTEN

MESSAGE FROM THE MEMOIRIST

As a continuator of the Robert Duncan, Charles Olson and Robert Creeley tradition, Paul is a reminder that the best writing comes from people who have lived life at the margins rather than in the safe confines of places like the Iowa Writer's Workshop. He spent time in the merchant marines, coming ashore in Vietnam in 1965 and 1966, and ran a jazz club called the Tin Palace later on. Every single poem in "Message from the Memoirist" reflects a lifetime of experience as a voyager...

—LOUIS PROYECT, COUNTERPUNCH

TITLES FROM MARSH HAWK PRESS

Jane Augustine, *KRAZY: Visual Poems and Performance Scripts, A Woman's Guide to Mountain Climbing, Night Lights, Arbor Vitae*

Thomas Beckett, ~~DIPSTICK~~ *(DIPTYCH)*

Sigman Byrd, *Under the Wanderer's Star*

Patricia Carlin, *Quantum Jitters, Original Green*

Claudia Carlson, *Pocket Park, The Elephant House*

Meredith Cole, *Miniatures*

Jon Curley, *Hybrid Moments*

Neil de la Flor, *An Elephant's Memory of Blizzards, Almost Dorothy*

Chard deNiord, *Sharp Golden Thorn*

Sharon Dolin, *Serious Pink*

Steve Fellner, *The Weary World Rejoices, Blind Date with Cavafy*

Thomas Fink, *Joyride, Peace Conference, Clarity and Other Poems, After Taxes, Gossip: A Book of Poems*

Norman Finkelstein, *Inside the Ghost Factory, Passing Over*

Edward Foster, *Dire Straits, The Beginning of Sorrows, What He Ought To Know, Mahrem: Things Men Should Do for Men*

Paolo Javier, *The Feeling Is Actual*

Burt Kimmelman, *Somehow*

Burt Kimmelman and Fred Caruso, *The Pond at Cape May Point*

Basil King, *The Spoken Word/the Painted Hand from Learning to Draw/A History 77 Beasts: Basil King's Bestiary, Mirage*

Martha King, *Imperfect Fit*

Phillip Lopate, *At the End of the Day: Selected Poems and An Introductory Essay*

Mary Mackey, *Travelers With No Ticket Home, Sugar Zone, Breaking the Fever*

Jason McCall, *Dear Hero,*

Sandy McIntosh, *Cemetery Chess: Selected and New Poems, Ernesta, in the Style of the Flamenco, Forty-Nine Guaranteed Ways to Escape Death, The After-Death History of My Mother, Between Earth and Sky*

Stephen Paul Miller, *There's Only One God and You're Not It, Fort Dad, The Bee Flies in May, Skinny Eighth Avenue*

Daniel Morris, *If Not for the Courage, Bryce Passage*

Sharon Olinka, *The Good City*

Christina Olivares, *No Map of the Earth Includes Stars*

Justin Petropoulos, *Eminent Domain*

Paul Pines, *Divine Madness, Last Call at the Tin Palace*

Jacquelyn Pope, *Watermark*

Karin Randolph, *Either She Was*

Rochelle Ratner, *Ben Casey Days, Balancing Acts, House and Home*

Michael Rerick, *In Ways Impossible to Fold*

Corrine Robins, *Facing It: New and Selected Poems, Today's Menu, One Thousand Years*

Eileen R. Tabios, *Sun Stigmata, The Thorn Rosary: Selected Prose Poems and New (1998–2010), The Light Sang As It Left Your Eyes: Our Autobiography, I Take Thee, English, for My Beloved, Reproductions of the Empty Flagpole*

Eileen R. Tabios and j/j hastain, *the relational elations of ORPHANED ALGEBRA*

Susan Terris, *Ghost of Yesterday, Natural Defenses*

Madeline Tiger, *Birds of Sorrow and Joy*

Harriet Zinnes, *New and Selected Poems, Weather Is Whether, Light Light or the Curvature of the Earth, Whither Nonstopping, Drawing on the Wall*

YEAR	AUTHOR	MHP POETRY PRIZE TITLE	JUDGE
2004	Jacquelyn Pope	*Watermark*	Marie Ponsot
2005	Sigman Byrd	*Under the Wanderer's Star*	Gerald Stern
2006	Steve Fellner	*Blind Date With Cavafy*	Denise Duhamel
2007	Karin Randolph	*Either She Was*	David Shapiro
2008	Michael Rerick	*In Ways Impossible to Fold*	Thylias Moss
2009	Neil de la Flor	*Almost Dorothy*	Forrest Gander
2010	Justin Petropoulos	*Eminent Domain*	Anne Waldman
2011	Meredith Cole	*Miniatures*	Alicia Ostriker
2012	Jason McCall	*Dear Hero*	Cornelius Eady
2013	Tom Beckett	~~DIPSTICK~~*(DIPTYCH)*	Charles Bernstein
2014	Christina Olivares	*No Map of the Earth Includes Stars*	Brenda Hillman

ARTISTIC ADVISORY BOARD

Toi Derricotte, Denise Duhamel, Marilyn Hacker, Allan Kornblum *(in memorium)*,
Maria Mazziotti Gillan, Alicia Ostriker, Marie Ponsot, David Shapiro,
Nathaniel Tarn, Anne Waldman, and John Yau.

For more information, please go to: **http://www.marshhawkpress.org.**